PREHISTORIC LIFE

THEODORE
ROWLAND-ENTWISTLE

🌸 BELITHA PRESS

First published in Great Britain in 1990 by
Belitha Press Limited
31 Newington Green, London N16 9PU
Copyright © Belitha Press Limited and
Gareth Stevens, Inc. 1990
Illustrations/photographs copyright © in this
format by Belitha Press Limited and Gareth
Stevens, Inc. 1990
ISBN 1 85561 011 6
Typeset by Chambers Wallace, London
Printed in the UK for Imago Publishing
by MacLehose and Partners

British Library Cataloguing in Publication Data
CIP data for this book is available from the British
Library

Acknowledgements

Photographic credits:

Bridgeman Art Library 9 top, 11 top
ET Archive 10
Geoscience Features 15, 20, 28
Robert Harding Picture Library 18, 47
Michael Holford 8/9
NHPA 23 top, 31, 37 top, 48 bottom
Natural Science Photos 5, 11 bottom, 14, 17, 19, 23
    bottom, 24 left, 29, 34, 35 bottom, 37 bottom, 41,
    48 top, 51, 56, 57 right
Nigel Press 7
Oxford Scientific Films 8 left, 12 top and bottom
    right, 33, 42, 44
Ann Ronan Picture Library 12 left, 13
Planet Earth 24 right, 26, 30, 32, 35 top

Illustrated by: David Holmes and Eugene Fleury

Series editor: Neil Champion
Educational consultant: Dr Alistair Ross
Editorial consultant: Neil Morris
Designed by: Groom and Pickerill
Picture research and art editing: Ann Usborne
Specialist consultant: the late Dr Gwynne Vevers

Contents

Words found in **bold** are explained
in the glossary on pages 60 and 61

1: PLANTS AND ANIMALS

Living Things Today

The world around us is teeming with living things. Some are plants, which cannot move about. Some are animals, most of which are able to move. Many more are tiny, simple living things which are neither plants nor animals, called protista. They include **bacteria** and the living organisms called **algae** which often form green slime on ponds.

There are about 350,000 different known kinds of plants and over a million kinds of animals. Each different kind of living thing is called a **species**. Biologists classify all these species to identify them and show how they are related. The system was worked out by the Swedish naturalist, Karl von Linné, in 1735.

Each species is given a Latin name. Latin names are used because many plants and animals have no common names. Many others

Hummingbirds live in North and South America.

The spotted souslik is a European ground squirrel.

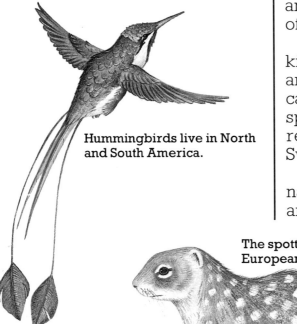

Starfish are a familiar sight in coastal waters.

The regal angelfish lives in tropical waters.

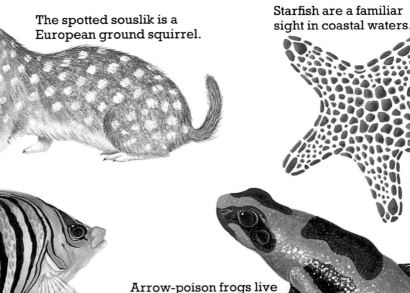

Arrow-poison frogs live in South America.

4

have the same common name. For example, at least eight different species of bird are called robins.

Living Things of Yesterday

For every species of plant and animal alive today there were ninety-nine more which lived in prehistoric times and are now extinct – that is, they have died out. One reason for this is that their places have been taken by new species. The process of forming new species is known as **evolution**. This has been going on for millions of years. The earliest known living things of the past were some algae whose remains have been found in rocks that are 3,800 million years old.

Evolution is still going on, but the process is so slow that we can hardly follow it. Some species have become extinct fairly recently – often because of human interference in the natural world. The mammoth died out only 10,000 years ago. The dodo, a flightless bird, died out in 1681. The passenger pigeon died out in 1914. Many other species are in danger, including the giant panda, Bengal tiger, orang-utan, river terrapin, far northern flax snail and the Chiapas slipper orchid.

▲ The orang-utan of Sumatra and Borneo is an endangered species. Only about 5,000 are left alive.

Many fungi are safe to eat, but others are poisonous.

Bugs like this one are destructive plant-eaters.

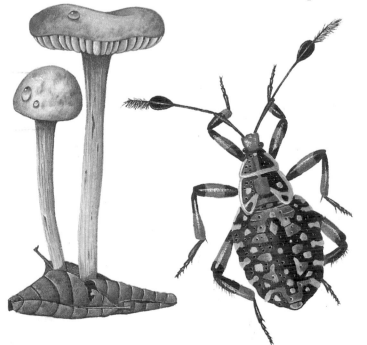

Classification

Classification consists of a series of ranks:

Kingdom: There are three kingdoms: animals, plants and protista (tiny organisms such as bacteria).

Phylum (plural phyla): All animals of the same basic type are grouped in a phylum. Example: chordates (animals with backbones) which include fish, birds and all the large animals (for plants, the word phylum is replaced by **division**).

Class: A more closely related group. Example: the mammals (animals that give their young milk) such as cats and cows.

Order: A sub-division of a class. Example: the carnivores (animals that eat flesh, such as cats).

Family: A sub-division of an order. Example: the cat family.

Genus: A sub-division of a family. Example: the big cats such as lions and tigers.

Species: Animals that really are alike. Every single lion alive is from the same species.

5

Earth: A Living Planet

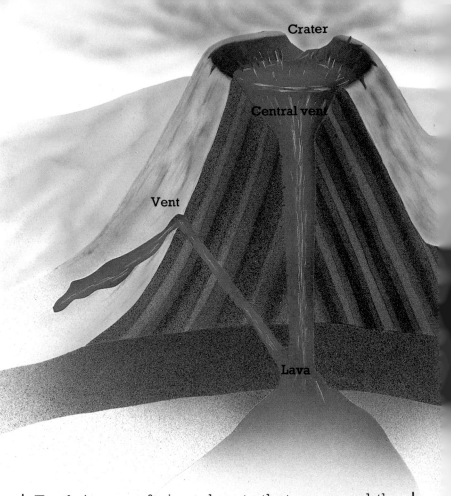

Crater

Central vent

Vent

Lava

► A volcano builds a cone of ash and lava around its central vent, where a crater forms. Another vent may erupt in the side of the cone.

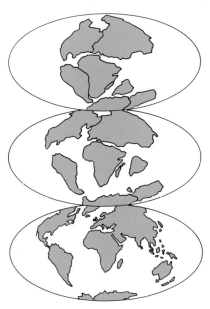

▲ The top map shows the continents as they were about 140 million years ago, about 60 million years after the supercontinent, **Pangaea**, broke up. The other maps show how they moved to their present position (bottom).

Earth is one of nine planets that go round the Sun. Space probes sent to land on other planets or fly close to them report that Earth is the only one which has life on it. The Earth itself also seems to be 'alive' as it changes all the time. The rock deep inside the Earth is so hot that it is **molten**. Some molten rock comes to the surface in volcanoes. There are also regions shaken by earthquakes, like Japan, Iceland and parts of the west coast of America.

The sea is always moving. It is lashed by fierce storms. Both rain and wind also wear away the land, in a process known as **erosion**. Rivers carry sand and mud from the land into the ocean.

Continents Divide

Many changes we can see taking place. But there are many more that happen so slowly that we do not notice them. A map of the world shows that the west coast of Africa and the east coast of South America look as though they

6

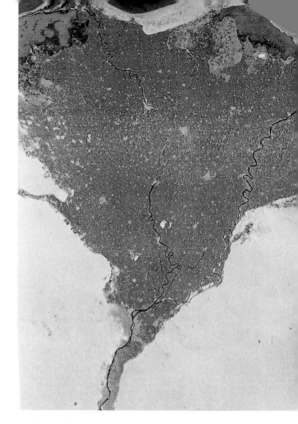

▲ A picture from a satellite showing the delta of the River Nile, built up over centuries by silt washed down the river. The computer-enhanced colouring shows clearly the area where plants are able to grow.

ought to fit together. About 135 million years ago they did exactly that. They were part of a huge supercontinent which we now call Gondwanaland. It also included Australia, Antarctica, and India. Gondwanaland broke up and the continents began to drift apart. They are still moving: every year, North America and Europe move about 5 centimetres (2 inches) farther apart. The surface of the Earth is covered by large **tectonic plates**, on which the continents sit. When two plates meet, one slides under the other, back inside the Earth. The upper plate is pushed upwards, making mountains. The Rockies, the Andes and the Alps were all made in this way.

Another slow change involves the level of the sea. A great deal of water is frozen and held in the ice caps that cover the North and South Poles. Those ice caps may vary in size. When they are large, the level of the sea falls, and more land is exposed. When the ice melts, the sea level rises.

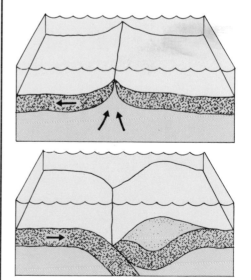

▲ The process of sea-floor spreading. Top, new material wells from volcanoes along the mid-ocean ridges, forcing the plates apart. Bottom – one plate sinks under another.

Stories of Creation

Most scientists today believe that all living things have evolved over millions of years. However, some people think that living things were created in their present form by God, or by many gods. People have always been curious about the origin of life and the world in which we live. They based their ideas on what they saw and believed to be true. For example, we know that the Earth goes round the Sun, but once people knew only that the Sun appears to move across the sky while the Earth stays still. The Earth is round but when people knew only a small part of the world they thought it was flat. When the huge bones of dinosaurs were first discovered, only a few hundred years ago, many people believed they were the bones of giant people.

Some Creation Legends

The Hebrew writers of the Book of Genesis said that God created Heaven and Earth out of a vast ocean. Hundreds of years earlier the people of Mesopotamia (now southern Iraq) believed the Earth and people were created as a result of a war between the gods.

American Indian legends of the creation also told of a vast sea. The Sun created land out of mud from the bottom of the sea. Some Pacific

▲ Evidence of ancient life is found in rocks. These bones at Dinosaur National Monument, Utah, in the United States, belonged to a dinosaur that lived between 225 million and 65 million years ago.

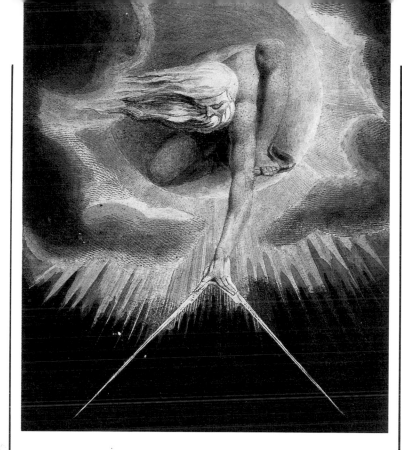

islanders thought at first there was a great emptiness, from which the world slowly came into being. The ancient Viking legends also spoke of a great emptiness, from which came the first living thing, a giant named *Ymir*. The god Odin killed Ymir, and formed the land and sea out of the giant's body.

Darwin's Discovery

H.M.S. 'Beagle', the ship in which Charles Darwin made a momentous voyage in the 1830s, anchored in a bay off Tierra del Fuego. His discoveries led to the theory of evolution by changes he called natural selection. ▼

In December 1831 a 22-year-old naturalist set off on a great adventure. Charles Darwin had been invited to join a scientific voyage around the world. He sailed in a small warship, *H.M.S. Beagle.* The voyage lasted nearly five years. During that time, young Darwin studied the plants, animals and geology of South America, Australia, New Zealand and the Pacific islands.

Darwin never travelled again, but in those five years he gathered enough information to help him form his theories of evolution. One thing that struck him was the great variety of different species he had seen. Where had they all come from? A number of other scientists were wondering that, too, but none of them had come up with a good answer.

Darwin was particularly interested in a group of birds called finches. He discovered them in the Pacific Ocean, on the Galápagos Islands, off the coast of Ecuador in South America. For this reason they are now called Darwin's finches. These finches are so alike

◀ Charles Darwin was barely 50 when this picture of him was painted. At the time, he was finalizing his theory of evolution. The geologist, Sir Charles Lyell (centre), and the botanist, Sir William Hooker (right), urged him to publish his work.

that they are obviously related. Yet they have different shaped beaks which help them to eat different kinds of foods – seeds, insects and the nectar of flowers.

Twenty Years of Thought

Darwin thought these finches must all be descended from just one kind of finch. He thought about the problem for nearly twenty years. He noticed that farmers could breed different kinds of cows, some to produce good meat, others to give rich milk. It seemed that just as the farmers could change the cows, natural processes could change the finches. He called the process of change **natural selection**. For example, one species of finch had developed a long thin bill, just the job for poking deep into flowers to drink the nectar.

Darwin's theories are still the basis for our ideas of evolution, and they help to explain how life developed in prehistoric times.

Over the centuries, farmers have bred many different kinds of cows from the original stock. Top, one of the Wild White Cattle of Chillingham, which are thought to be like the originals; bottom, a Jersey Cow. ▼

◀ The medium ground finch, one of Darwin's finches from the Galápagos Islands, has a short beak suitable for eating seeds. Some of Darwin's finches have long, slender beaks.

Searching for the Past

Scientists today are constantly learning more about prehistoric life and evolution. They are finding many remains of past life preserved in rocks, and have discovered how to calculate the age of those rocks and remains.

Present-day research into evolution uses the science of **genetics**. This theory was put forward by an Austrian monk named Gregor Mendel. Mendel experimented by crossing short and tall varieties of peas, and found that some of the resulting plants were tall and others short.

Other scientists following up Mendel's work found that features such as height, skin, hair and eye colour are determined by parts of the cells that make up the body of an animal or plant. These parts are called **genes**.

These two pictures show the ▶ two colours of the peppered moth. In the upper picture, the normal light moth is harder to see on a clean tree than the dark one. In the lower picture the light moth shows up clearly against sooty bark, and the dark moth does not.

▲ Gregor Mendel spent his life in the monastery at Brno, Czechoslovakia, and eventually became its abbot.

◄ Mendelian inheritance of colour in peas is shown here. On the left are pink flowered peas, and on the right, white ones. In the middle are flowers of a cross between the two, containing mixed colouring.

Leaps and Bounds

Darwin thought that changes were gradual, and built up to produce different species. Many scientists now think that though gradual changes are indeed going on all the time, there are also sudden jumps in evolution.

An example of gradual evolution is shown by two varieties of an insect, the peppered moth. In the clean air of the countryside the peppered moth is light in colour, and when it rests against the bark of light-coloured trees it is almost invisible to hungry birds. But in towns where the air is sooty the bark of trees is black. There, a dark variety of the peppered moth flourishes, because in those circumstances it is also hard to see.

Survival

Some people make the mistake of supposing that changes such as that of the peppered moth take place in order that the moth can survive. In fact the moth survives *because* it has changed and so matches its new background.

In the same way, wasps avoid being eaten by birds because they are poisonous. Hoverflies also survive because they are black and yellow and look very like wasps. This is known as **protective coloration**.

Protective coloration: The mountain king snake, on the left, is harmless, but other animals avoid it because it looks like the highly poisonous coral snake, on the right. ▼

2: CLUES TO THE PAST

Reading the Story

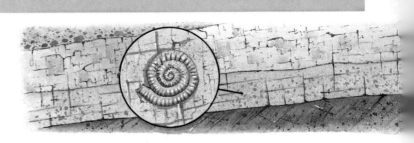

Rock strata laid down over ▶ many years, in a wall of the Grand Canyon in Arizona, in the United States.

Some of the story of the past has been preserved in the rocks that make up the Earth's crust, its outer layer. With care and skill we can read quite a lot of that story in the rocks. There are three basic kinds. Some have come welling up from inside the Earth, all hot and molten. They are called **igneous rocks**. Others are made up of tiny pieces of rock, like sand, that have been laid down in water. The fragments have stuck together and hardened to form fresh rock: called **sedimentary rocks**, because they are formed from sediments. The third kind is formed when existing rocks, igneous or sedimentary, are changed by heat, pressure and chemical action inside the Earth. These rocks are called **metamorphic rocks**.

Glomar Challenger

Since 1968 a special drilling ship, the American *Glomar Challenger,* has been taking cores from the sea-bed, deep under the oceans. These cores have told us a lot about the Earth's history, and have also helped in the search for oil.

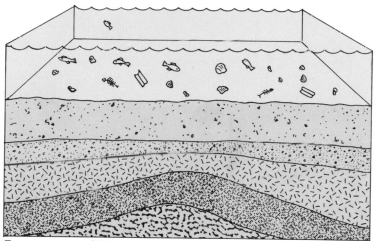

Layers of Rock

Our rock 'book' is made up of the sedimentary rocks. These rocks are formed over many millions of years, and are laid down in layers, known as **strata**.

Usually the top layer is the newest and the bottom layer is the oldest. But sometimes great movements of the Earth's crust over a long time can fold these rocks so that they lie at an angle, on edge, or even turn upside down with older layers on top of newer ones.

Many sedimentary rocks contain the remains of animals and plants that lived when the rocks were being laid down. Chalk is a kind of rock that is formed almost entirely from the shells of very tiny creatures that lived in the sea during the Cretaceous Period.

▲ Here you can see different layers of rock. They are laid down at different times over millions of years. Fossils are found in them.

◄ Deposits of oil and natural gas can become trapped under layers of rock. Here, a layer of impervious (waterproof) clay prevents oil from leaking upwards from a porous layer of rock, which has been lifted and folded. Oil is formed from the bodies of tiny prehistoric sea animals.

▲ Drill **cores** from samples deep in the ground, lying in long troughs that are known as coffins.

15

Fossils

This is how layers of fossils are found in the Earth's crust. The time scale has been condensed: in reality the layers would not be so close together. By matching up fossils found in different places, geologists are able to say in what period the animals lived. ▼

We know about prehistoric life because the remains of many plants and animals have been preserved as **fossils**, usually in sedimentary rocks. Some fossils are only a few thousand years old, but others were formed many millions of years ago.

Most fossils are formed when the remains of an animal or plant becomes buried in sand or silt, usually in watery places such as swamps, river beds or in shallow seas close to the shore. Over a long time more silt piles on top, and becomes stone (see pages 14-15).

Fossil Formation

There are four main ways fossils are formed. Some have been turned to stone, some are moulds or casts, some are traces, and a few are whole animals or plants.

Stone fossils are formed in several ways. A dead animal's bones and shell may become filled with minerals from the water into which it has sunk. The minerals harden to form stone. The bone or shell survives reinforced with this

stone. Water may dissolve away the body of a plant or animal, and minerals replace it. We have a stone replica of the original. Or the soft parts of plants or animals decay and a carbon print of the original plant or animal survives in the stone. Often a print is not found until the stone is split.

Sometimes the dead animal or plant just dissolves away, leaving a hollow mould fossil. This may fill with minerals to form a stone cast of the original.

Ancient Footprints

A trace fossil is a mark left by a long-dead creature. Typical trace fossils are footprints, left in mud which has since hardened. Often it is difficult to decide which animal made the traces.

Very rarely we find a whole animal or plant preserved. Insects or other small creatures are occasionally found preserved in amber. Amber is fossilized resin, the clear sticky stuff which oozes from some trees.

▲ This fossil fish lived in the Cretaceous period, (140 million to 65 million years ago).

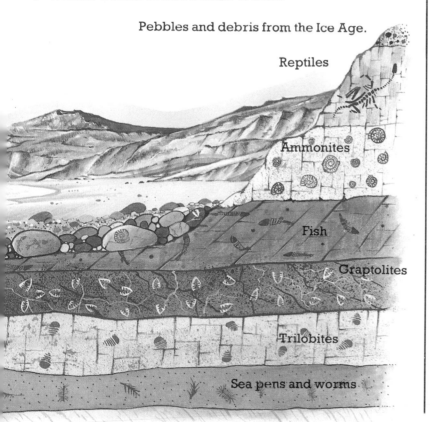

Pebbles and debris from the Ice Age.

Reptiles

Ammonites

Fish

Graptolites

Trilobites

Sea pens and worms

Living Fossils

● The **coelacanth** is a primitive kind of fish thought to be extinct for 65 million years until one was caught off South Africa in 1938.

● The **ginkgo** is a kind of tree native to China and Japan. It is the only survivor of a group of plants that flourished 200 million years ago.

● **Horsetails** are primitive plants that have changed little in 300 million years.

● *Neopilina* is a limpet-like mollusc which was known only from fossils 350 million years old – until a live specimen was found in the Pacific Ocean in 1952.

● The **tuatara** is a New Zealand lizard which is the sole survivor of a group of reptiles that were common 200 million years ago.

● The **Virginia opossum** of the USA has changed hardly at all in the past 64 million years.

Finding Fossils

Fossil logs 200 million years ▶ old lie scattered over the desert floor in Petrified Forest National Park, Arizona. Fossil trees, whose wood has turned to stone, can be found in many parts of the world.

Famous Sites

● The **Dinosaur National Monument** on the borders of Utah and Colorado in the USA contains rich fossil remains of dinosaurs and other prehistoric animals.

● **Fossil trees** can be seen in the Petrified Forest National Park, Arizona, USA and also in the Glasgow Museum in Scotland.

● **Neanderthal**, or Neander Gorge, near Düsseldorf, West Germany, is the site where the first skull of Neanderthal Man was found.

● **Olduvai Gorge**, Tanzania, contains many fossil remains of early people, some of them around 2 million years old.

● **Rancho La Brea**, near Los Angeles, is the site of tar pits where thousands of animals were trapped in pools of tar during the Pleistocene Period over 2 million years ago.

Fossils can be found almost anywhere there are exposed sedimentary rocks. Good places to look are cliffs by the sea or by rivers, and in the walls of quarries. Fossils are also found in coal-mines. Indeed, coal itself is a fossil. It is the remains of forests which grew in the Carboniferous Period.

It is not enough just to collect fossils. Notes must be taken of exactly where and in which layer of rock they were found. Otherwise the full story of the rock and its fossils cannot be read and recorded.

◄ Collecting fossils can be a time-consuming task requiring a great deal of patience. Here, a collector is brushing dirt off an ichythyosaur – a marine reptile with a body like a porpoise – before he numbers the bones to identify them.

A Matter of Life or Death

It is important to note what other fossils are found nearby. For example, human skeletons near an assortment of animal bones may show what our distant ancestors ate. Sometimes fossils are found in the place where they lived. A group of fossils found together like this is known as a **life assemblage**. But often you find an untidy heap of fossils, especially fossil shells. A heap of this kind was generally formed when the sea or a river washed the shells together after the owners were dead, just as you find empty shells on the beach today. Such a group is known as a **death assemblage**.

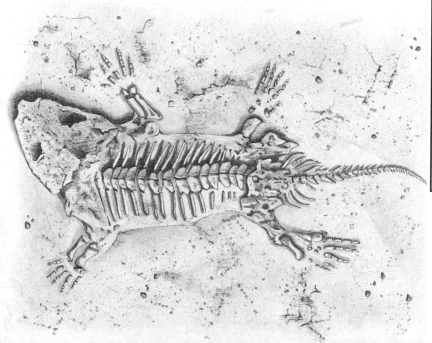

Beware!

If you go fossil hunting yourself, go with somebody who knows about it. It can be dangerous. Close to cliffs and in quarries you should always wear a hard hat for protection against falling rocks. By the sea you must keep a look-out for incoming tides that can trap you.

Dating Rocks

Geologists use **radioactivity** as one way to calculate the age of rocks. Many rocks contain **elements** such as uranium, thorium and potassium. As these give off radioactivity they slowly change into other elements. The speed at which they decay has been worked out (it is very slow). Scientists know how much radioactivity there should be in new rocks. So by measuring how much radioactivity is left in old rocks they can work out their age.

◄ Finding the fossil remains of long-dead animals can be very exciting, especially when they are complete

Rebuilding Fossils

Finding and excavating a fossil is only part of the story. It needs great skill and knowledge to put a collection of scattered bones back together to build up a skeleton. Some early attempts to reconstruct dinosaurs were quite wrong, but that was because no complete skeletons had then been found. The scientists had to guess what the missing parts were and how the bones had fitted together in life.

A lot depends on how carefully the fossils are dug out. Accurate notes, photographs and drawings must be made to show how the bones were lying when found.

Males and females of the same species are often of different sizes. Male elephants are larger than females, and female spiders are larger than male spiders. Similar differences have sometimes misled scientists into thinking they had found fossils of two separate species.

Cleaning and Repairing

Rebuilding a fossil skeleton may take months of work in a laboratory. Workers clean the bones. They put broken bones together and may reinforce them with steel rods. If some

The Iguanodon

A fossil may be completely misleading. For example, a cone-shaped bone of the dinosaur *Iguanodon* was found in the early 1800s. People thought it was a horn like that of a rhinoceros. Then in 1878 a patch of sand full of huge bones was found in a Belgian coal-mine. The complete skeletons of more than 30 *Iguanodon* were dug out and reassembled. The 'horn' turned out to be the animal's thumb bone.

A diorama – a three-dimensional picture – showing plants and animals of the Cretaceous Period, 65-140 million years ago. The animals include dinosaurs and pterosaurs – flying reptiles with wings of skin, like bats, more than 5 m (16 ft) across. ▶

bones are missing they may make plaster or fibreglass copies of other bones. For example, if the bones of one foreleg are found the other foreleg will normally be a mirror image of it.

Sometimes it is possible to make a lifelike model of a prehistoric animal. Scientists who study anatomy (the structure of animals) know what sort of muscles are likely to fit on a skeleton. The skin may be a matter of guesswork. The great cave bear, for instance, probably had skin and fur much like modern bears. Extinct reptiles are likely to have had skin similar to that of modern reptiles.

The skeletons displayed in museums of prehistoric animals like the iguanodon (left) and the crocodilian (right) are reconstructed. Putting a fossil skeleton together is like doing a three-dimensional jigsaw puzzle, often with some pieces missing. ▼

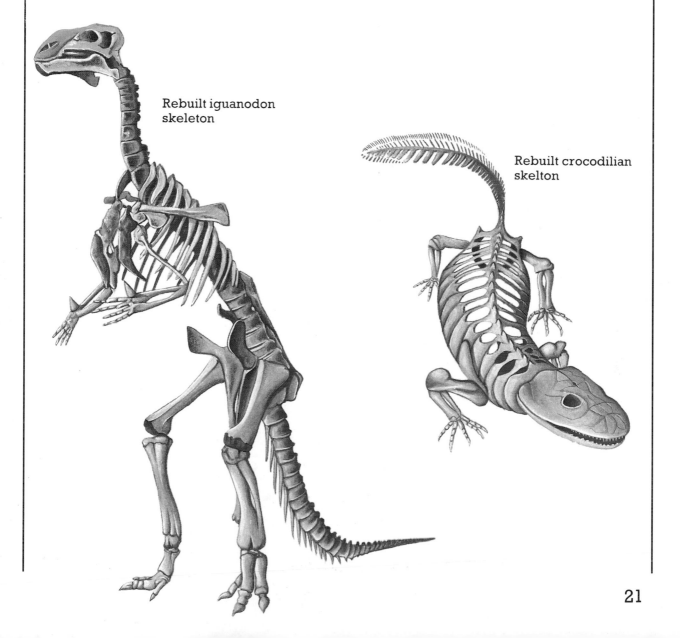

Rebuilt iguanodon skeleton

Rebuilt crocodilian skelton

3: LIFE IN THE OCEANS

The Early Days

In its early days, the Earth had many volcanoes, which erupted clouds of steam and gases. As with present-day volcanoes, there were often violent thunderstorms at the same time. The steam condensed to form rain, which gradually filled up the oceans with water. ▼

The oldest known rocks are in Western Greenland, and they are estimated to be 3,570 million years old. The Earth is about 4,600 million years old. What happened in the first 1,000 million years? We have been able to work out the likely course of events from clues left in the rocks, and from what is happening today.

In its early days the Earth had a great many volcanoes. These volcanoes hurled out lava and rock. They also pumped out great quantities of steam and other gases. The steam slowly turned into water to form the oceans, probably just over 4,000 million years ago.

The other gases released by the volcanoes included many of the gases that we find in the atmosphere today. At first there was very little

oxygen, a gas that is essential for life. It was all locked up in the ocean, because water consists of the two gases, hydrogen and oxygen.

A Gradual Build-up

Light and heat from the Sun began to break up some of the ocean's water and release oxygen. A layer of oxygen slowly formed. It included **ozone**, a form of oxygen which cuts off most of the more harmful rays of the Sun. Without this ozone, living things would burn up. A few forms of plant life evolved in shallow pools, deep enough under water to be safe from the Sun's rays. They began to make their own food, as plants still do, by a process known as **photosynthesis**.

Photosynthesis also releases oxygen into the atmosphere. So, very slowly the plants built up the Earth's supply of oxygen in the air.

In time there was enough oxygen and ozone – about one tenth of the present amount – for plants to survive near the surface of the oceans, as the microscopic plants of the **plankton** still do. This happened about 600 million years ago, just before the period of Earth's history we call the Cambrian.

▲ Top, a young, rugged mountain – Machapuchare in Nepal; bottom, an older mountain, partly worn away – a peak in the Mlange Massif, Malawi.

Life Begins

Life could not begin on land because in the early years of the Earth there was not enough oxygen in the atmosphere (see pages 22-23). So it seems certain that life began in the oceans.

For long enough, scientists thought life depended only on the heat and light of the Sun, which plants use for **photosynthesis**. But in the 1970s fishes, giant worms and crabs were discovered living in one of the deepest parts of the sea, more than $2\frac{1}{2}$ kilometres ($1\frac{1}{2}$ miles) below the ocean surface. The Sun's rays cannot reach such depths.

These animals feed on bacteria which grow in hot water that wells up from cracks in the sea-bed. So the necessary energy comes from inside the Earth. It seems likely that the earliest forms of life started in much the same way.

Earliest Evidence

Some of the earliest evidence for life comes from Australia. There geologists have found some bun-shaped rocks, called **stromatolites**,

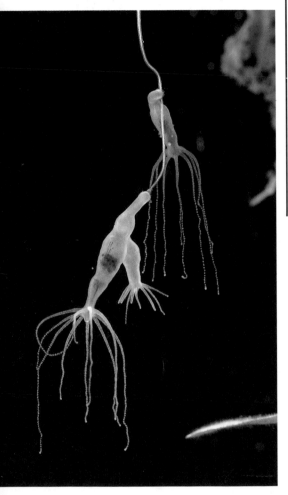

▲ A hydra, a simple freshwater animal whose ancestors probably evolved at the same time as stromatolites were formed.

A female deep-sea angler fish ▶ with two parasitic males. Bony fish evolved less than 150 million years ago.

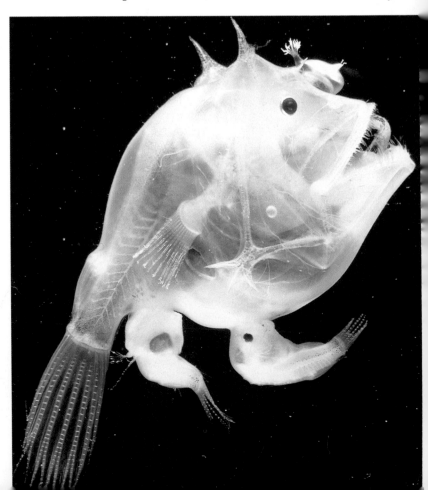

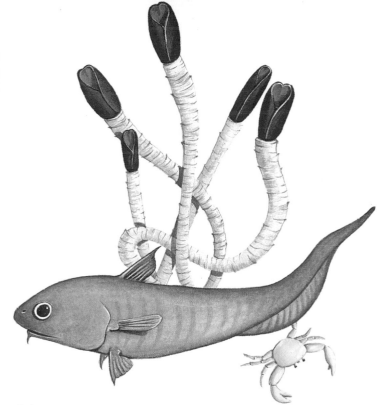

◀ Crabs, fish and giant worms have been found deep in the ocean. They get their food from bacteria which flourish in hot water welling up from cracks in the ocean floor.

which are about 3,500 million years old. Stromatolites are built up by very simple organisms called **blue-green algae**. These algae form slimy layers on rocks and wet ground. They belong to the kingdom Protista (see pages 4-5). Similar algae have been found in 2,000-million-year-old rocks in Minnesota.

These and other early forms of life were all simple one-celled organisms. The oldest multi-celled animals so far discovered were some fossils in rocks in Australia and Newfoundland. These fossils belong to creatures that lived in Precambrian times, about 700 million years ago. They include jellyfish, various kinds of worms, and creatures related to starfishes.

Fossilized sea animals that lived long ago. They are all examples of the simple creatures, such as worms and jellyfish, which were among the earliest known ocean dwellers. ▼

Dickinsonia, **a worm**

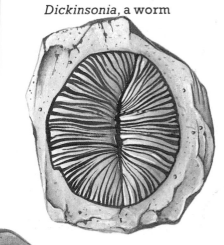

Charnia, **a sea pen**

Medusina, **a jellyfish**

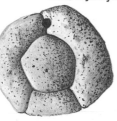

Spriggina, **a worm**

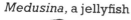

Animals without Backbones

Jellyfish, like this one, are found in all the oceans of the world. ▼

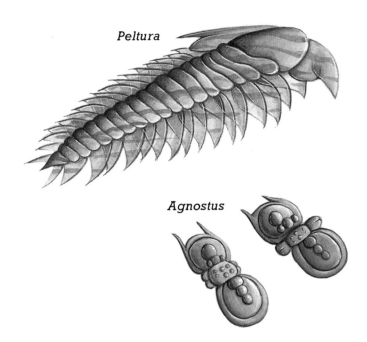

Peltura

Agnostus

The Sea Scorpion

One of the most terrifying pre-historic marine animals was the giant sea scorpion, *Pterygotus*. This extinct relative of modern scorpions was over 2 metres (6¼ feet) long. It had six pairs of limbs – a pair of claws, four pairs of legs for walking, and a pair of paddles for swimming.

Invertebrates

The period from the late Precambrian to the beginning of the Devonian is sometimes called *The Age of Marine (sea) Invertebrates,* because invertebrates were for most of that time the only animals in the sea. **Invertebrates** are animals without backbones. Even today there are many times more invertebrates than vertebrates, animals with backbones.

In Precambrian times all these marine animals had soft bodies. For this reason, we have few fossil remains, except **trace fossils** that show where the animals crawled across the sea-bed or burrowed into it.

Early in the Cambrian Period, animals began to develop hard parts – shells, chalky tubes and chalky external skeletons. These hard parts fossilise readily, so we have a much better idea of animal life from Cambrian times onwards.

Trilobites

One of the most common sea animals of this period of Earth's history was the trilobite, a small creature with a hard shell. Trilobites belonged to the **arthropods**, a group that in-

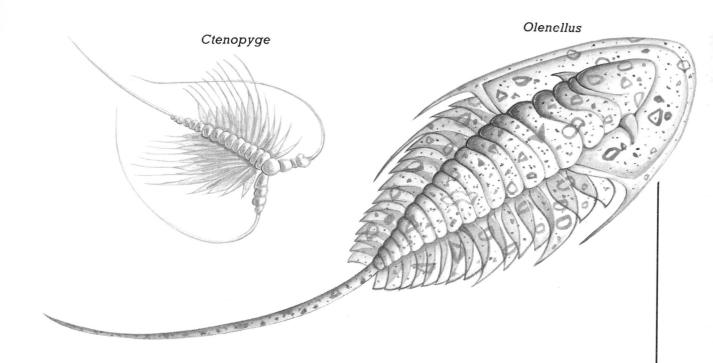

Ctenopyge

Olenellus

cludes present-day spiders, insects and crustaceans. They flourished for about 370 million years. There were more than 10,000 species.

Molluscs of the Past

There were also many molluscs in the sea. Living molluscs include snails, limpets, oysters, scallops and octopuses. Fossil molluscs include animals similar to many present-day species.

Two kinds of mollusc no longer exist but are common as fossils. Ammonites were molluscs with coiled shells. They lived from the Devonian Period to the end of the Cretaceous Period. They varied in size size from less than 2 centimetres (1 inch) across to 2 metres ($6\frac{1}{2}$ feet). Their shells were divided into chambers which were filled with air or gas. The only similar kind of mollusc today is the nautilus.

Belemnites had bullet-shaped shells, known to the people who first found them as 'the Devil's thunderbolts'. Their soft parts were probably a bit like those of the present-day cuttlefish.

Invertebrates Who's Who

Invertebrates are grouped into more than 20 **phyla** (see page 5). Here are some of the most important:

- **Sponges**.
- **Jellyfishes and corals**.
- **Comb jellies and sea gooseberries**.
- **Molluscs:** such as ammonites, clams, limpets, octopuses, oysters, snails, slugs.
- **Earthworms, leeches and lugworms**.
- **Arthropods:** the mixed group of creatures that includes mites, scorpions, spiders, barnacles, crabs, crayfish, lobsters, shrimps, insects, horseshoe crabs, trilobites.
- **Brittle stars, sea cucumbers, sea urchins, starfish**.

Animals with Backbones

The development of backbones was a major step forward in evolution. The **vertebrates** – animals with backbones – include nearly all the biggest, most active and intelligent animals. There are very few vertebrate species compared with the rest. For every one there are 27 invertebrate species.

Many invertebrates have their skeletons outside their bodies, like the hard casing of a beetle. The problem with an external skeleton is that it is like a suit of armour – it does not stretch. If the animal grows it has to moult, or shed its outer casing. It has a new, larger-sized soft casing underneath, which quickly hardens to become the new skeleton.

Vertebrates belong to a larger group called the chordates. The three other kinds of chordates live in the sea. They do not have a true backbone, but instead have a primitive supporting rod, called a notochord. They include acorn worms, sea squirts and lancelets.

A vertebrate has its skeleton inside its body, so it never needs to moult. The skeleton grows with its body. Most skeletons are made of hard, strong bone, but two groups of fishes,

▲ A typical vertebrate bony skeleton, that of a gorilla.

Diorama of animals, plants and landscape of the Jurassic period. ▶

28

including lampreys and sharks, have softer, tough cartilage (gristle) instead of bone.

Hard Outer Cases

A few vertebrates, such as turtles, armadillos and some dinosaurs, developed hard bony plates or shells which give protection. The main nerves of a vertebrate's body run inside the backbone. At the head end the nerves enlarge to form the brain, which is protected by the skull. Another feature of vertebrates is skin, which almost entirely covers the body.

Because vertebrates have strong internal skeletons, many have been able to grow much bigger than invertebrates. This is very important for land animals, because air does not give their bodies support as water does. The development of the brain enables vertebrates to do more complex things than invertebrates, which do not have true brains.

We know very little about the evolution of vertebrates. The earliest surviving vertebrate fossils are of some primitive fishes related to modern lampreys and hagfishes. They date from Cambrian times (570 million years ago).

▲ A bull shark, a species that lives in tropical seas.

Vertebrates Who's Who

There are seven classes of vertebrates. They belong to the **phylum** Chordata (see page 5).

● **Lampreys and hagfishes**: fishes which do not have jaws.

● **Sharks and rays**: fishes with cartilage (gristle) instead of bone.

● **Bony fishes**: all the other important and common fishes.

● **Frogs, toads, newts and salamanders**: the amphibians, which live partly in water and partly on land.

● **Reptiles**: crocodiles, lizards, turtles and snakes, and in the past the dinosaurs.

● **Birds**.

● **Mammals**: all the animals which feed their young on milk, from mice to elephants.

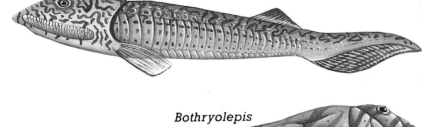

Cephalaspis

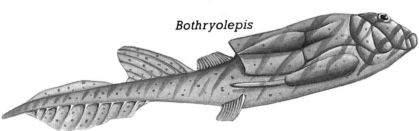

Bothryolepis

Fishes

Tricky Fossils

Fish give us another example of the need to think carefully about the fossils we find. One group of fossil fishes was found with their bodies lying in a curve instead of flat. At first people thought this curved shape suggested the fish had been poisoned. Then it was realised that when dead fish dry they often contract into a curve like this.

A blue-spotted ray, a typical cartilaginous fish. ▼

The first fishes swam in the seas some time in the Cambrian Period. They were jawless fish. They were also the first vertebrates and were very simple in structure. Because they had no bones, only **cartilage**, they left few fossils. There are two kinds of jawless fish still living: hagfishes and lampreys.

Four classes of fish with jaws appeared in the Silurian Period. Two classes, which had thorny skin and plated skin, are now extinct. The other classes survive to this day. All four groups lived in the Devonian Period. That period is often called the *The Age of Fish* because that was when fish began to dominate the oceans, as they still do.

Fish with cartilage instead of bone belong to the class Chondrichythes (see page 29). Modern fishes of this class are the sharks and

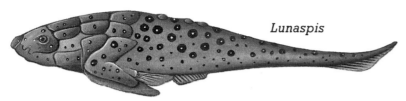

Jamoytius

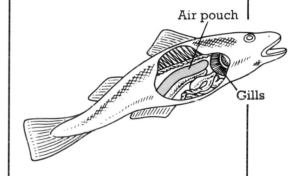

Lunaspis

◀ Fishes of the Silurian and Devonian periods. *Cephalaspis* and *Jamoytius* were jawless fishes (like modern lampreys); *Bothryolepis* and *Lunaspis* were early jawed fishes.

Rays. Unlike other kinds of fish, sharks and rays do not have air pouches to help keep them afloat. But they do have plenty of fat, which is lighter than water.

Keeping in the Swim

Generally speaking a shark keeps afloat by swimming forward. If it stops swimming it sinks. It can turn and change depth quickly but cannot swim backwards.

There are more bony fishes than any other vertebrates, in the sea or on land. There are many thousands of fossil fishes, some of which are quite unlike modern fish. However, deep-sea divers are continually finding unknown species of fishes. So one day we may come across another fish we thought was extinct, like the coelacanth (see page 17).

▼ Anatomy of a fish.

Air pouch

Gills

A surgeon fish. This fish is of the bony type and lives among coral reefs. ▼

4: LIFE COMES ASHORE

Land Plants and Animals

Frogs (opposite page) emerged around 200 million years ago. A modern descendent is the red-eyed leaf frog, found on the Caribbean coast of Costa Rica. ▶▶

The West African lungfish is a modern relative of the early lungfish which were the first vertebrates to venture on dry land. This animal spends the hot summer months sheltering in mud. ▼

Millions of years ago plants and water animals moved from the salt seas to the fresh water of rivers. Marine plants were simple, one-celled organisms. The first large plants we know of grew in swampy areas and peat bogs. These were water plants, with their roots under water and their tops in the air. They flourished about 400 million years ago.

Within 100 million years, plants had spread from the swamps to cover a large area of the land. As they grew and spread they pumped more oxygen into the atmosphere, making life on land easier.

The first land animals were probably animals with jointed limbs – ancestors of today's insects, spiders and crustaceans.

▲ Labyrinthodonts get their strange scientific name from the structure of their teeth. They were early amphibians, looking something like present day salamanders. Many were very large animals. They died out about 190 million years ago.

Leg-like Fins

The first vertebrates to venture on land were lungfishes. These fishes, some of which still exist, lived in rivers and freshwater lakes. As well as the gills that other fish use for breathing in water, lungfish have lungs to breathe air. Some modern species cannot breathe in water. Their fins are a bit like legs. The fish can use them for 'walking' on the river bed, or to drag themselves over land.

After the lungfish came the **amphibians**. Frogs are amphibians. They lay their eggs in water and the young, known as tadpoles, live and breathe in water. As they mature they grow legs, come on to land and breathe air.

Amphibians developed in the Devonian Period. For more than 100 million years they were the dominant land animals. Some pre-historic amphibians were quite large – up to 4 metres (13 feet) long – though others were only about 30 centimetres (1 foot) long.

These and many other kinds of amphibians are now extinct. But three groups of amphibians still survive: frogs and toads, newts and salamanders, and caecilians, wormlike amphibians which have no legs.

Amphibians Who's Who

There are three groups of amphibians living today. These are:

● **Frogs and toads**: they make up the order *Salientia*, which means 'jumping animals'. They have long back legs which enable them to jump. The adults do not have tails.

● **Newts and salamanders**: make up the order *Caudata*, which means 'having tails'. These animals have tails as well as legs.

● **Caecilians**: form the order *Apoda*, which means 'legless'. They have no legs, and are slim, worm-like creatures that live in the tropics.

Changing

▲ Even a bare wall can provide a habitat for mosses and lichens.

A polar bear roams the Arctic snows. It has a thick layer of blubber (fat) under its heavy fur which means that it can survive even in temperatures of −37° C (34° F). ▼

Animals moved from the water and became adapted to life on land (see pages 32-33). We need to understand this in order to realise how prehistoric life evolved.

Worms burrow into the ground, and their slim, flexible bodies seem the ideal shape for pushing through the soil. Many birds sleep perched in trees. Their legs are so constructed that when the birds relax, their claws grip the branch on which they are perching more tightly, so the birds cannot fall off.

It is easy to think that the worm and the bird have developed in order to burrow and perch. But what really happens in evolution is that a creature develops some quality that adapts it for a certain way of life.

A Place in the World

Every plant and animal has its place in the world. **Ecologists** (scientists who study the relationships between organisms and where they live) call such places **niches**. The term 'niche' refers not only to the actual place but to such things as the food that is available or the climate.

Some niches are very general. A rabbit, for example, will do well almost anywhere where there is a good supply of grass and other greenstuff to eat. Others are very specialized.

◀ Koalas live in eucalyptus trees in the forests of eastern Australia. They feed on the leaves of the trees, and rarely eat other plants.

Two lions, a male and a female, charge through the African grassland. Lions often work in groups to hunt animals such as antelopes and zebras, with the lionesses doing most of the work. ▼

A koala lives and feeds only on certain eucalyptus trees, cacti flourish in deserts and mangrove trees grow only in swamps.

Scientists have found that differences in species develop most quickly in islands or other isolated places. Charles Darwin noticed that in the Galápagos Islands, fourteen species of finch had evolved, each able to find and eat a different kind of food (see pages 10-11).

Scientists think that all these finches are descended from a few birds that landed on the islands between 5 million and 10 million years ago. The birds that did best in each of fourteen ecological niches are the ones that flourished and have left the most descendants.

Tool for a Bird

One of the finches Darwin saw, the woodpecker finch, has a trick that very few birds have. It uses a tool to get its food. The finch has a short, stout beak with which it chops its way into the bark of trees to get at insect grubs. But it does not have a long tongue nor a slim enough beak to winkle the grubs out of their burrow. So it uses a small twig or a thorn from a cactus to pull the grubs out. Very few birds use tools in this way.

Coal Forests

▲ An artist's impression of what the Carboniferous tropical forests probably looked like. Giant ferns, horsetails and club mosses grew as tall as trees. Their roots were in swamps, just like mangrove trees of today.

Kinds of Coal

There are several different kinds of coal. They vary according to how and when they were formed. The most plentiful is bituminous coal, which breaks into large rectangular blocks. Anthracite is the hardest coal, because it was formed deep down at great pressure. Lignite or brown coal has been formed most recently and at shallower depths.

During the Carboniferous Period, much of the land that is now Europe, Asia and North America was covered by tropical swamps. Forests of giant trees grew in these swamps. Most of the trees were very different from modern forest trees.

Some trees were club-mosses. Today, club-mosses are just small moss-like plants, but in the Carboniferous Period, some club-mosses grew into massive trees more than 30 metres (100 feet) tall. Other common trees in those prehistoric forests were giant ferns and horsetails.

We know about these forests and their plants because their remains have survived as the coal we dig out of the ground and burn.

When plants die in damp places, such as swamps, they rot to form a thick layer of decaying vegetable matter. This is like you might find in the lower layers of a garden compost heap.

Coal Formation

In time this layer becomes buried under later layers, and compresses and heats up to form peat. Peat is the first stage in the formation of coal. There are huge areas of peat in the USA, Canada, Finland, Germany, Britain, Ireland and the Soviet Union.

In the prehistoric swamps the beds of peat were buried by layers of sand or mud as rivers rose and washed over them. When the land dried out again more forests grew, to decay and form further layers. This is why we find coal in seams, layers ranging from a few centimetres to many metres thick, separated by layers of rock formed from the sand and mud. Fossils of marine plants and animals are sometimes found in the rock layers, showing that the forests grew close to the sea coast, probably in river estuaries.

In among the coal we find the fossil remains of bark, seeds, cones and other plant debris. There are also fossil insects and other small creatures. Sometimes the coal is in the form of charcoal, showing that trees were slowly burned in a prehistoric forest fire.

▲ Tree ferns still grow in tropical lands. These tree ferns are in a forest in Malaysia.

Peat, an early stage of coal formation, is found in swamps in many parts of the world. Here, people are digging it out to be dried and used as fuel. ▼

Cones and Flowers

Ferns, horsetails and club mosses, which formed the Carboniferous forests, all reproduce by means of **spores**. Spores can be seen underneath the fronds on present-day ferns.

Some trees of today were already in existence, and have been around since Devonian times. They were trees like **conifers**, such as spruce, larch or pine trees. They bear seeds, plain to view, in cones. When they are ripe, the seeds have little wings. The wind blows them away, to land on the ground and start new trees.

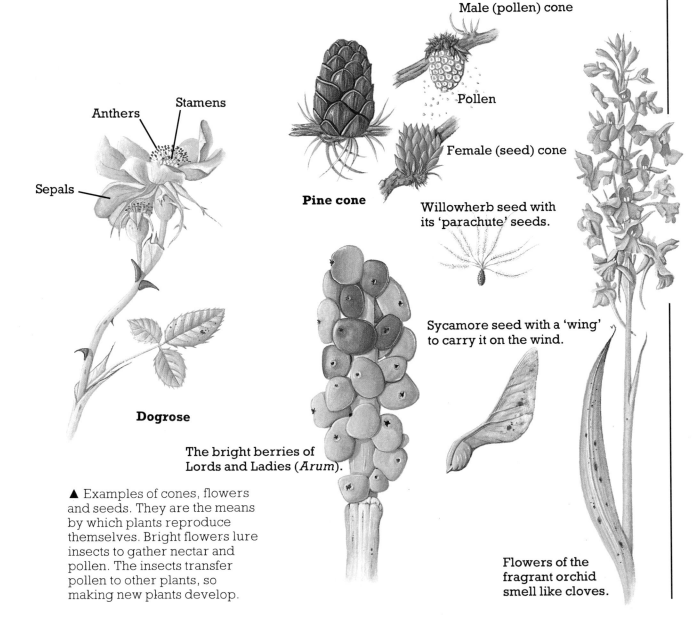

Stamens

Anthers

Sepals

Dogrose

Male (pollen) cone

Pollen

Female (seed) cone

Pine cone

Willowherb seed with its 'parachute' seeds.

Sycamore seed with a 'wing' to carry it on the wind.

The bright berries of Lords and Ladies (*Arum*).

Flowers of the fragrant orchid smell like cloves.

▲ Examples of cones, flowers and seeds. They are the means by which plants reproduce themselves. Bright flowers lure insects to gather nectar and pollen. The insects transfer pollen to other plants, so making new plants develop.

Flowers Take Over

These 'naked-seed' trees formed the world's main forests for about 200 million years. Then, just over 100 million years ago, in the Cretaceous Period, there was a botanical 'explosion'. This was the arrival of the flowering plants. Their seeds are hidden inside fruit. Within a short time (geologically speaking) flowering plants spread all over the Earth. They were very successful in evolutionary terms. We do not know when the first flowering plants evolved. The oldest known is a tiny bloom found preserved in Cretaceous mud in Sweden.

This plant revolution changed the appearance of the Earth completely. It also brought about a major change of food for the animals of the time.

Two groups of animals have evolved in close association with flowering plants. Insects carry pollen from one flower to another, while large vegetarian mammals, such as cattle, depend on grasses and other flowering plants for their food. Although mammals have existed since the Triassic Period, they became Earth's dominant animals only after the development of flowering plants. So we see how one form of prehistoric life depended on another.

You can tell how successful flowering plants have been because there are more than 236,000 living species today. By contrast, there are only 665 living species of the naked-seed plants.

▲ Left, the outer case of a chestnut splits open to reveal the ripe seed (the nut) inside. Above, a section through a daffodil shows the stamens and the pistil deep inside.

▲ Insects are attracted to plants but this plant eats insects. It is a sundew.

5: REPTILES

Rulers of the Earth

▲ A duck-billed dinosaur and a small horned dinosaur of the Cretaceous period.

▼ Skeleton of a dinosaur partly reconstructed to show how it fed.

Reptiles were the first true land vertebrates. The earliest reptile fossils are found in rocks 300 million years old. It is probable that reptiles are descended from amphibians. One big difference between amphibians and reptiles is in the eggs they lay. The eggs of amphibians, like those of other water animals, are soft and have to be **fertilized** in water after they are laid. The eggs of reptiles and birds are enclosed in a **membrane** or skin, and are fertilized before they are laid. In birds and many reptiles the egg has another outer casing, a hard shell. Shell and membrane stop the egg from drying out, but allow the egg to 'breathe' – oxygen can enter from the air and carbon dioxide from inside can leave.

Ancestors of the Mammals

The earliest reptiles were shaped something like stocky crocodiles. In the Permian and early Triassic periods, the dominant animals were a group known as the mammal-like reptiles. Some were very small, but others were as large as a rhinoceros. These mammal-like reptiles died out in the Triassic Period. They left behind their descendants, the first **mammals**.

Those early mammals were very small. The real rulers of the Earth throughout the Mesozoic Era were the reptiles. Two groups took over from the mammal-like reptiles. One group formed the lizards and their descendants, the snakes. The early lizards were mostly insect eaters.

The second group are known as archosaurs, which means 'ancient lizards'. The archosaurs lived near rivers and the seashore. They spent a lot of their time in the water, hunting for fish which formed their main food.

Some of these archosaurs developed a sprawling way of walking. They were the ancestors of present-day crocodiles. The other archosaurs developed long, powerful hind legs and short front legs, like those of kangaroos. They were the ancestors of the dinosaurs.

▼ Snakes were the last group of reptiles to evolve. Few fossils are found because their skeletons are so fragile. This Californian mountain kingsnake is lying in the sunshine, warming up and getting ready to go and hunt for food.

◄ When temperatures are high, reptiles rest in the shade to prevent themselves from overheating, like this Nile crocodile. Crocodiles were well established by about 200 million years ago and their shape has hardly changed. ▼

The Dinosaurs

Bird-hipped Dinosaurs

There were many extraordinary shapes among the bird-hipped dinosaurs. Some had hard plates and spines on their backs that protected them against the flesh-eaters. *Stegosaurus* had plates standing up like a fish's fins. *Triceratops* and some others had horns like those of a rhinoceros.

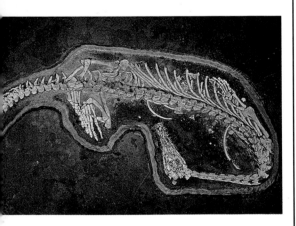

▲ The fossil skeleton from Brazil of a *Mesosaurus*, a small dinosaur which lived part of the time in water.

▶▶ Some of the many kinds of dinosaurs which flourished in the Age of Reptiles. Slender-winged pterosaurs fly overhead.

During the time from the Triassic to the Cretaceous Periods the climate of all the land areas of the Earth was warm and moist. At that time the land was all one huge supercontinent, known as Pangaea (see pages 52-53). Dinosaurs lived all over this supercontinent for 140 million years. This supercontinent split, to form Gondwanaland in the south and Laurasia in the north.

The dinosaurs came in all sorts of shapes and sizes. The smallest of these reptiles were about the size of a present-day chicken. But many dinosaurs were very big indeed.

The largest was *Ultrasaurus*. It was the biggest animal that ever lived on land, and was 35 metres (115 feet) long from nose-tip to tail-tip. With its long neck it was tall enough to look over a present-day three-storey house.

Giant Vegetarians

There were two basic kinds of dinosaur. We can tell them apart by the shape of their hip bones. One group had hips like modern lizards. The other group had bird-like hips.

The lizard-hipped dinosaurs included both meat-eaters and plant-eaters. Some, such as *Diplodocus* and *Brachiosaurus*, were huge, slow-moving plant-eaters which walked on all fours. The flesh-eaters, including the fierce *Tyrannosaurus rex*, walked on their hind legs. They had sharp claws with which they tore their prey, and long teeth.

The bird-hipped dinosaurs evolved later than the lizard-hipped dinosaurs. Like their lizard-hipped cousins some, such as *Iguanodon*, walked on their hind legs. They included the hadrosaurs, which had a bill like that of a duck – but with up to 2,000 teeth in it.

Modern reptiles are cold-blooded – their blood is at almost the same temperature as the air around them. They have to warm up in the sun, or cool off in the shade or in water. Mammals and birds, which are warm-blooded, have a steady body heat. Some scientists think dinosaurs were warm-blooded.

Rhamphorhynchus

Apatosaurus

Tyrannosaurus Rex

Lesothosaurus

Compsognathus

Deinonychus

Prolercerta

Swimming and Flying Reptiles

An ithyosaur leaps and dives after fish, while a long-necked plesiosaur swims under water. In the sky, a flock of pteranodons, large pterosaurs with 5 m (16 ft) wingspans, glide and dive, also hunting fish. ▶

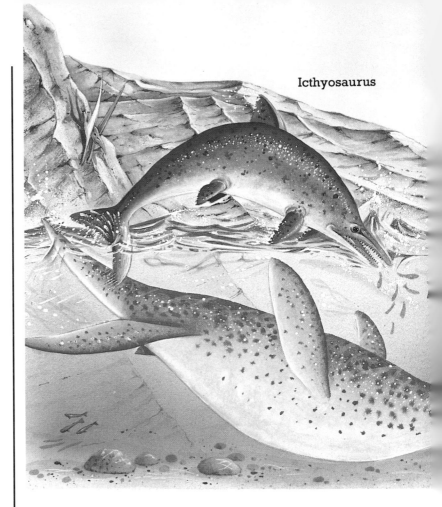

Icthyosaurus

▲ Turtles have existed for about 200 million years. Even the earliest known fossils had complete upper and lower shells, like those of modern turtles, such as this Atlantic loggerhead turtle.

Dinosaurs paddled about in swamps, and crocodiles swam in rivers and in shallow seas just like their modern descendants. But some prehistoric reptiles swam in the oceans, as whales and porpoises do today. There were two kinds: ichthyosaurs, which means 'fish-lizards', and plesiosaurs, which means 'near-lizards'.

The 'Winged Lizards'

While ichthyosaurs and plesiosaurs took to the sea, other reptiles took to the air. They are known as pterosaurs, which means 'winged lizards', or pterodactyls, meaning 'winged fingers'.

The first reptiles to take to the air were gliders, like the flying squirrels of today. They lived in trees and 'parachuted' from one tree to another, or to the ground. They lived in the Triassic Period. The 'parachute' was formed by two membranes of skin. One linked

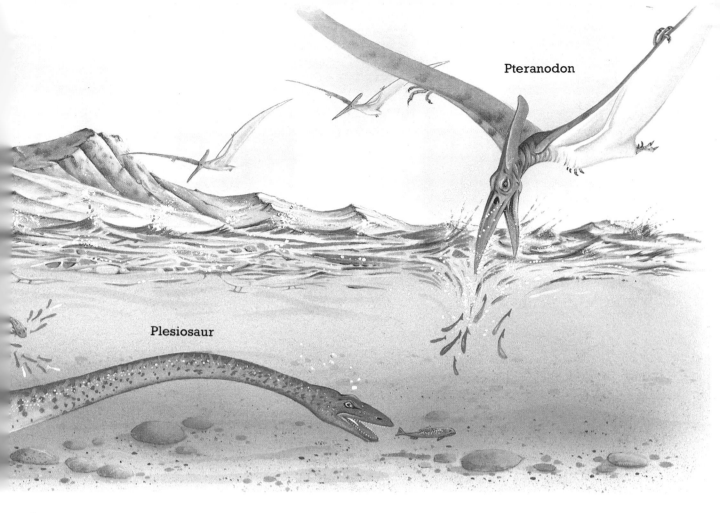

Pteranodon

Plesiosaur

the elbows and knees, the other ran from the ankle to part way down the long tail. Remains have been found in the Soviet Union.

The true pterosaurs had wings of skin, similar to those of modern bats. In 1971 the fossilized skeleton of one pterosaur was found in the Soviet Union, complete with its skin. The skin was hairy, and scientists think the pterosaurs were warm-blooded animals. Early pterosaurs had teeth in their beaks, and long tails. Later ones did not.

The smallest pterosaurs were about the size of a sparrow. The largest pterosaur was *Quetzalcoatlus,* a vulture-like reptile with a wing span of 10 metres (33 feet). That is about three times the wing span of the wandering albatross, the bird with the biggest wing span today. Another huge pterosaur was *Pteranodon,* which had a wing span of 7.5 metres (25 feet. *Pteranodon* had no tail, but had a long bony crest on the back of its head for balance.

Did You Know?

The ichthyosaurs had streamlined bodies like those of dolphins, and they paddled their way through the water. They had long jaws and lots of teeth. They never came to shore to lay eggs, but gave birth to live young in the water, just as whales do.

Plesiosaurs had barrel-shaped bodies, and they swam through the water with a flying motion, rather like penguins. One group of plesiosaurs had very long necks, and small heads with sharp teeth. They fed on fishes. Another group had short necks and large heads with blunt teeth. They and the ichthyosaurs ate fish and shellfish. At least some of the plesiosaurs seem to have been able to move on land.

Extinction

Mass Extinctions

The fossil record shows that there have been at least six mass extinctions in the past 500 million years. The two most dramatic occurred in the Permian and the Cretaceous Periods.

The first extinction took place slowly over many millions of years. It killed eight out of ten species of marine creatures.

The Cretaceous extinction, the one that killed the dinosaurs, was much faster, and may have lasted only a few thousand years.

Other mass extinctions, about which we know little, occurred in the late Ordovician, about 440 million years ago; the mid-Devonian, about 370 million years ago; the late Triassic, about 200 million years ago; and about 2 million years ago.

Although there are millions of species of animals alive today, many more existed in the past and have become extinct. Apart from natural disasters, which might have caused the mass extinctions, the reason for animals becoming extinct is that they are no longer suited to the conditions in which they are living. ▶

One of the biggest mysteries of prehistoric life is what killed the dinosaurs? After ruling the Earth for 140 million years they then died out. There are no fossils of dinosaurs later than about 65 million years ago.

The dinosaurs died out in what is known as a **mass extinction**. A great many other species died out at the same time, including the flying and swimming reptiles, the pterosaurs, ichthyosaurs and plesiosaurs. The ammonites, which had been a feature of ocean life since the Devonian Period, also vanished. Yet many kinds of animals survived, including amphibians, birds, corals, crocodiles, mammals, snakes and turtles.

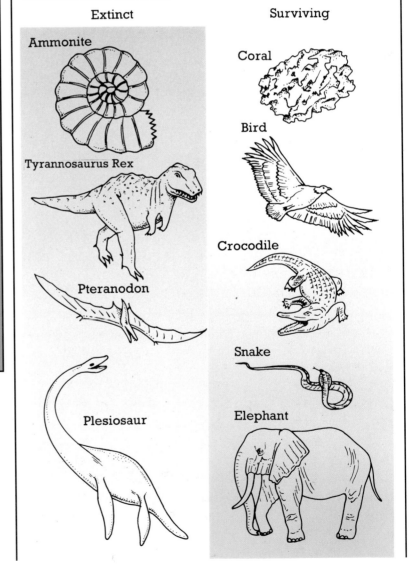

Extinct — Ammonite, Tyrannosaurus Rex, Pteranodon, Plesiosaur

Surviving — Coral, Bird, Crocodile, Snake, Elephant

◀ The huge cloud of ash and debris that rose from Mount St Helens, in Washington State, USA, in May 1980. But although that produced darkness over a wide area, it was a tiny disaster compared with the eruption of Mount Tambora in Indonesia in 1816, whose dust clogged the world's skies for a whole year.

Killed by Plants?

Another possible cause of the end of the dinosaurs was the development of flowering plants (see pages 38-39). Some people think that the dinosaurs were used to eating other kinds of plants and could not digest the flowering plants, just as giant pandas eat only bamboo shoots.

Change of Climate

Some scientists think that a huge meteorite hit the Earth and changed the climate. The meteorite would have sent up a cloud of dust, which could block out the Sun for several years. Even a large volcanic eruption, such as that of Mount St Helens (USA) in 1980, can send up a cloud of dust that affects the weather. Other scientists think that perhaps a comet flew close by the Earth, heating up the atmosphere.

The most likely explanation is that a big change in the Earth's climate was caused by a lowering of the sea level and the movement of the continents (see pages 52-53). Towards the end of the Cretaceous Period, many land areas that were once in the warm tropics had moved north into colder parts of the Earth.

One clue is that fossil remains of dinosaurs show they lived later in the **tropics** than they did in what are now the **temperate** parts of the Earth. Even if the dinosaurs ate the flowering plants, such plants tend to die back in temperate winters. This would leave little food for the huge animals for months at a time.

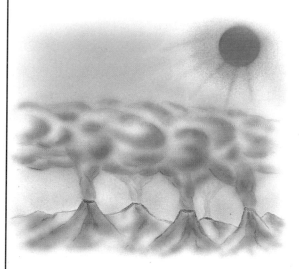

▲ One theory about the mass extinction of the dinosaurs is that the climate changed suddenly. This may have been caused by a huge **meteorite** crashing into the Earth, sending up clouds of dust that would have blocked out the Sun.

Birds

▲ An artist's impression of what *Archaeopteryx* probably looked like. We have no idea what colour it was.

The Fish-Bird

Ichthyornis, the Fish-Bird, whose fossils come from the same area as those of *Hesperornis*, was only about 20 cms (8 ins) tall. It probably had no teeth. It was like modern gulls and terns in shape and habits.

▶ *Archaeopteryx* may have climbed trees in order to take off, like this starling flying from its nest.

Birds are descended directly from reptiles. We are lucky enough to have five fossils of what may well have been the very first bird. They were found in Germany. This ancestral bird is called *Archaeopteryx*, which means 'ancient wing'.

Archaeopteryx was about the size of a pigeon. It had feathers like a modern bird, but it had heavy bones like a reptile. It was almost certainly too heavy to fly, but it may have climbed trees and glided. It had teeth. Its ancestor was probably not one of the flying reptiles, but the chicken-sized reptile *Compsognathus*. Like *Compsognathus*, *Archaeopteryx* probably sprinted along the ground to catch the insects and other small animals on which it fed.

Few fossils of birds have been found from later periods. But they show that within 10 million years of *Archaeopteryx* all the features of birds as we know them had evolved. These features include lightweight, hollow bones, toothless beaks, and a big breastbone that supports the wing muscles.

The Dawn Bird

Many of the early birds had teeth. Among them was *Hesperornis*, the Dawn Bird, a flightless water-bird whose fossils have been found in the Great Plains of North America. *Hesperornis* was shaped like a modern diving bird, and some were about 2 metres (6 ft) long. It had 94 teeth.

Even today birds have many features that are like those of reptiles. The most obvious is the scales on the legs of birds such as chickens. They are similar to the scales found on reptiles.

The Flightless Bird

Fossils of several giant birds have been found. They include *Diatryma*, a flightless bird. One specimen stood 2 metres (6½ feet) tall. It lived in what is now North America between 60 million and 40 million years ago. *Diatryma* had a heavy, parrot-like beak.

Birds of many different types existed in the past that are no longer around today. ▼

Diatryma

Ichthyornis

Hesperornis

Archaeopteryx

Mammals

▲ This is an artist's impression of an early mammal. We do not know what many of them would have looked like.

Did You Know?

Mammals now number more than 4,200 species. They are grouped into 18 orders. As with the reptiles, some mammals are flesh-eaters, and some eat only plants.

After the extinction of the dinosaurs, the Earth was dominated by birds and mammals. A **mammal** is an animal which gives birth to live young and suckles them on their mother's milk. The early mammals fed at night, partly because the dinosaurs, who were mostly much bigger, foraged for food during the day.

The first mammals appeared in the Triassic Period. They were small, shrew-like animals.

There were many **marsupial mammals**, animals with pouches like a modern kangaroo. Marsupials give birth to young that are not fully formed. The young climb into the mother's pouch to finish developing. The rest, called **placental mammals**, give birth to fully developed young.

The Isolated Marsupials

The placental mammals were more successful than the marsupials. The marsupials survived only in Australia and South America, where they were cut off from their rivals, the placental mammals (see pages 52-53).

About 64 million years ago the mammals began to move into new regions. Many species evolved that have since become extinct, such as the mammoth and the great cave bear. It is interesting that horses developed first in North America. Yet they died out there after spreading to other parts of the world, until humans took them back 400 years ago.

A number of mammals have taken to life in the seas. They include whales, dolphins and porpoises, which never come to live on land, and seals and their relatives, which give birth to their young on land. The earliest known whale fossils are about 50 million years old, and the oldest seal fossils date back about 20 million years.

Mammals Who's Who

There are 18 orders (see page 5) of mammals. They are:

● **Egg-laying mammals**, such as the platypus.

● **Marsupials**, the pouched mammals, such as kangaroos and opossums.

● **Insect eaters**, such as hedgehogs, shrews and moles.

● **Flying lemurs**, which glide rather than fly.

● **Bats**, the only mammals which flap their wings to fly.

● **Primates**, the lemurs, lorises, monkeys, apes and man.

● **Sloths and anteaters**.

● **Pangolins**.

● **Hares and rabbits**.

● **Rodents**, the gnawing animals, such as rats, mice, beavers and squirrels.

● **Dolphins, whales and porpoises**, the sea mammals.

● **Carnivores**, the meat-eaters, such as cats, bears, wolves and seals.

● **The aardvark**.

● **Elephants**.

● **Hyraxes**.

● **Sea-cows**.

● **Odd-toed hoofed animals**, such as horses, tapirs and rhinoceroses.

● **Even-toed hoofed animals**, such as pigs, camels, cattle, deer, sheep, goats and hippopotamuses.

◄ Woolly mammoths probably looked like this. Complete bodies have been found in Siberia, perfectly preserved. The last mammoths died out only about 10,000 years ago.

51

Moving Continents

The continents have not always been where they are now. At the end of the Triassic Period, they were joined together to form the super-continent Pangaea (see pages 6-7).

During the Jurassic Period they broke apart. Over millions of years, the Atlantic Ocean opened up. North America and Europe moved apart, and so did South America and Africa. To the south, Australia, Antarctica and the Indian subcontinent broke away from Africa. This movement of the land is called **continental drift**.

Continental drift had an enormous effect on prehistoric life. Pangaea lay much further

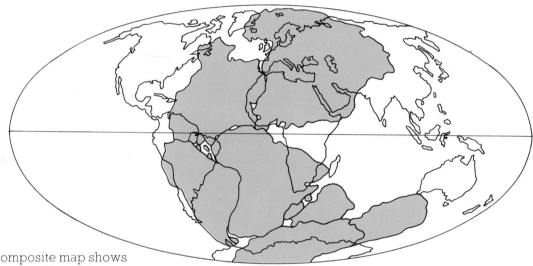

▲ This composite map shows the present location of the continents, and how they fitted together to form the supercontinent Pangaea.

south than most of the land does today. The climate over most of Pangaea was warmer and more even than the world climate is today. It was in this environment that the dinosaurs flourished. As Pangaea broke up and continents became smaller, the climate grew colder. Many plants and animals found it difficult to adapt to the new conditions.

Animals in Isolation

One important result of continental drift was that a number of plant and animal communities became isolated. Australia had **marsupial mammals** and no **placental mammals** when it became isolated.

Drifting Dinosaurs

Dinosaur fossils show the effect of continental drift. At the end of the Jurassic Period the plated dinosaur *Stegosaurus* died out everywhere except in India, where they lived on for another 50 million years or so. During this time India was drifting in isolation towards Asia, where eventually it collided. The collision forced up the great Himalayan mountain range.

Duck-billed platypus

Tasmanian wolf

Kangaroo

As a result the marsupials developed to fill all the **ecological niches** (see pages 34-35) that were occupied by the other mammals elsewhere. So we have marsupial mice and cats, kangaroos instead of deer or antelopes and Tasmanian wolves instead of grey wolves. Primitive egg-laying mammals, like the duck-billed platypus and the echidnas, also survived in Australia and its near neighbour, New Guinea.

South America was another island. It was not linked to North America until just over 2 million years ago. It too had marsupials, and a number of placental mammals such as giant ground sloths and plant-eating animals that looked like rhinoceroses. One group of South American marsupials, the opossums, still survives, and has spread to North America.

▲ Marsupials, such as the kangaroo and the opossum, are descended from ancient stock which survived in the isolated continents of Australia and South America. The two species of sloths that survive today in South America are all that survive of a large group that included the megatheres, giant ground sloths.

Humans Arrive

The figures from left to right show the development of hominids, from the ape-like *Australopithecus* to modern Man, known as Cro-Magnon Man, from the site in France where the skeletons were first found. ▼

When Charles Darwin first published his *Origin of Species* in 1859 (see pages 10-11) many people thought he was claiming that people were descended from monkeys – which Darwin was not saying.

Three things distinguish hominids from apes: they walk upright, use tools, and communicate with each other by means of language. Fossil skulls can sometimes show whether their owners could speak or merely grunt. The shape of the leg bones shows if they walked upright. The earliest hominid fossil so far found was discovered in 1981 in Ethiopia. It is about 4 million years old. It belonged to *Australopithecus*, meaning 'Southern Ape'. The earliest fossils belong to the species *afarensis*. Three other species of *Australopithecus* have been discovered in southern and eastern Africa: *A. africanus*, which lived about 3 million years ago and *A. robustus* and

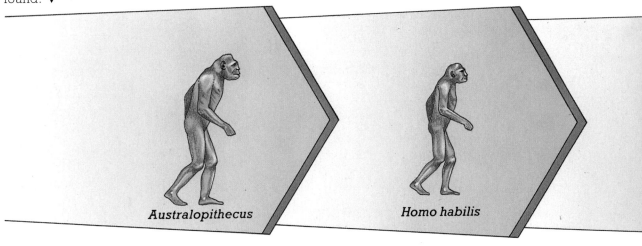

Australopithecus

Homo habilis

A comparison of the skull of modern Man, *Homo sapiens*, with those of other hominids. The skull of Neanderthal Man looks very similar to that of modern Man, and that is because Neanderthal Man was a sub-species, whose scientific name is *Homo sapiens neanderthalensis*. The word 'Man' with a capital M is used here to indicate a species, including both sexes. ▶

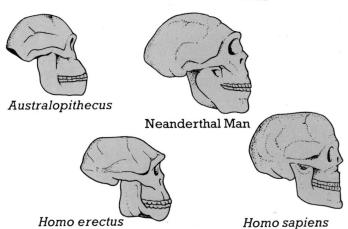

Australopithecus

Neanderthal Man

Homo erectus

Homo sapiens

A. boisei, which lived about 2 million years ago and made simple stone tools.

Humans belong to the genus *Homo,* which means 'Man'. The earliest human was *Homo habilis* ('Handy Man'), who lived in East Africa about 1,800,000 years ago, at the same time as *Australopithecus boisei.*

Fossils of *Homo erectus* ('Upright Man') have been found all over the world. The earliest specimens were found in China and Indonesia. At first they were known as 'Peking Man' and 'Java Man'. Upright Man made better stone tools, and used fire. He roamed the Earth for 1,300,000 years.

Finally, about 300,000 years ago, Upright Man died out and his place was taken by *Homo sapiens* – 'Wise Man'. A strong, rugged form of Wise Man, Neanderthal Man, lived in Europe during the Ice Age, from about 75,000 to 35,000 years ago.

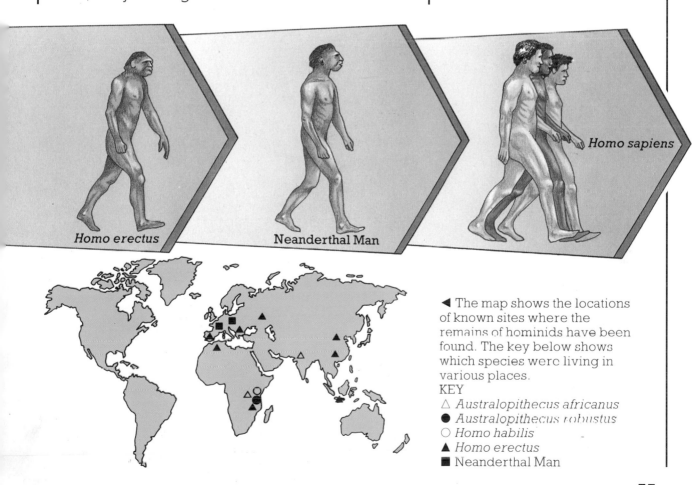

Homo erectus

Neanderthal Man

Homo sapiens

◀ The map shows the locations of known sites where the remains of hominids have been found. The key below shows which species were living in various places.
KEY
△ *Australopithecus africanus*
● *Australopithecus robustus*
○ *Homo habilis*
▲ *Homo erectus*
■ Neanderthal Man

BIRDS AND MAMMALS

The Future

The study of prehistoric life shows us three things. Firstly, that humans evolved very recently in terms of **geological time** – the whole period of Earth history. Secondly, that the changes we call evolution take place extremely slowly as far as our own idea of time is concerned. Thirdly, that evolution is still going on.

In an incredibly short time, geologically speaking, humans have come to dominate the Earth. We have a much bigger effect on our world than even the dinosaurs did. People change the landscape wherever they go.

We are cutting down tropical forests at the rate of 12 hectares (30 acres) a minute, 24 hours a day. By doing so we are destroying the **ecological niches** where millions of insects and other animals live. If we are not careful, we shall cause a catastrophe as great as the two biggest mass extinctions (see pages 46-47). A nuclear disaster like the one which took place at Chernobyl, in the Soviet Union, in 1986 could also cause world-wide damage to all life on Earth.

The Galápagos Islands in the Pacific Ocean are a unique habitat, providing ecological niches for species not found elsewhere. They include the Galápagos fur seals and the swallowtailed gulls seen here. ▼

Did You Know?

New species of plants and animals are evolving now, though the process is so slow that we do not realise it is going on. There are more species alive today than there have ever been. Some, we know, are becoming extinct.

◀ Many plants are rare, such as this Chinese slipper orchid. Fortunately, people are now aware of this, and efforts are made to preserve such plants, and in many cases their habitats.

Forest in Celebes, in Indonesia, is being cleared for human settlement, with the loss of plants and animals. ▼

Genetic Engineering

Already plant and animal breeders are able to 'improve' species to help farmers. Now, by a process called **genetic engineering**, scientists are learning how to alter the cells of which organisms are made. This is likely to produce even greater changes in plant and animal life.

Our own future development may be changed if people establish colonies on the Moon or other planets. Research in Hawaii and the Galápagos Islands shows that new species develop most rapidly in island communities. Colonies on other planets would be island communities on a large scale. Perhaps in a few million years there will be a new species of *Homo*.

Meanwhile we learn more every year about how plants and animals have evolved in the past. In time we may even find out how life itself began.

The Ages of the Earth

ERAS	PERIODS		MILLIONS OF YEARS AGO
PRECAMBRIAN (Before the Cambrian)		The longest period, about seven times as long as all the rest put together. It is sometimes divided into two sub-divisions, the Proterozoic, or time of the earliest forms of life, and the Archaean, or ancient time.	4600
PALAEOZOIC (Ancient Life)	CAMBRIAN	The oldest period of the Palaeozoic Era. Its rocks were first identified in Wales, and its name comes from *Cambria,* the Latin name for Wales. Fossils from this period include many marine animals, including the first primitive fish.	570
	ORDOVICIAN	The second period of the Palaeozoic Era. Its name comes from the *Ordovices,* a Celtic tribe that lived in Wales. Again, the animal life was in the sea. It included the trilobites.	500
	SILURIAN	The third period of the Palaeozoic Era. It is also named after a Celtic tribe, the *Silures.* Its marine animal life included the trilobites and the sea-scorpions.	435
	DEVONIAN	The fourth period of the Palaeozoic Era. It is named after the English county of Devon, where many rocks of this period are found. Fish became the most important animals in the sea. The first land plants and animals existed in this period.	395
	CARBONIFEROUS	The fifth period of the Palaeozoic Era. Forests of giant tree-like ferns and horsetails flourished and their remains formed the coal. The period's name comes from carbon, the main substance of coal. Nearly all the world's land was in the southern hemisphere at this time, and a large South Polar ice-cap formed.	345
	PERMIAN	The most recent period of the Palaeozoic Era. It is named after Perm, in the Ural Mountains of the Soviet Union, where its rocks were first identified. Amphibians, reptiles, mammal-like reptiles and modern kinds of insects flourished. There was a mass extinction at the end of the period which killed off many sea animals, including the trilobites.	280

The Earth's long history is divided into four main lengths of geological time, called eras. Each era is divided into periods, and the two most recent periods are divided into series. They are all shown on the Geological Time Chart here.

ERAS	PERIODS	SERIES		MILLIONS OF YEARS AGO
MESOZOIC (Middle Life)	TRIASSIC	The first period of the Mesozoic Era. It is named after a triple sequence of rocks laid down at this time. Large reptiles, including the early crocodiles and dinosaurs, flourished, and the first mammals lived at this time.		230
	JURASSIC	The second period of the Mesozoic Era. It takes its name from the Jura Mountains between France and Switzerland. This was the age of the dinosaurs, while the mammal-like reptiles died out. The earliest-known bird, *Archaeopteryx,* lived towards the end of the Jurassic.		195
	CRETACEOUS	The last period of the Mesozoic Era. It is named after the chalk (Latin *creta*) that was laid down at this time. Dinosaurs were still dominant, while pterosaurs (flying reptiles) and primitive birds flew through the air. At the end of the Cretaceous there was another mass extinction that killed off the dinosaurs (see pages 46-47).		140
CENOZOIC (Recent Life)	TERTIARY	Palaeocene	Tertiary and Quaternary make up the Cenozoic Era. Their names are left over from an 18th-century division of geological time, in which the Palaeozoic Era was called Primary, and the Mesozoic Era was Secondary. They are divided into series, and include all the developments of the past 65 million years.	65
		Eocene		54
		Oligocene		38
		Miocene		22.5
		Pliocene		5
	QUATERNARY	Pleistocene		2
		Holocene		0.01

Glossary

Algae: (singular alga) Simple plants that live in seawater and fresh water. Some are made up of just one cell; others, the seaweeds, have many cells.

Amphibian: An animal that can live on both land and in water.

Arthropod: Literally 'jointed feet'; any member of a phylum of invertebrates that includes insects, spiders, crustaceans, centipedes and millipedes.

Bacteria: (singular bacterium) Simple one-celled organisms, a few of which can cause diseases.

Blue-green algae: The simplest kind of algae, which form slime on rocks and in ponds.

Cartilage: Gristle, a rubbery tissue found in the bodies of vertebrates.

Chemical element: Any of the basic substances from which everything is made.

Class: A rank of animals or plants that comes between a phylum or division and an order.

Conifers: A type of tree that has cones; usually evergreen.

Continental drift: The movement of the continents across the Earth, which has been going on for the past 200 million years.

Core sample: A long cylinder of rock, obtained by drilling down into the Earth's crust.

Death assemblage: A group of fossils that have come together after death.

Division: The equivalent for plants of a phylum

Ecological niche: The place or conditions in which a plant or animal lives.

Ecologist: A scientist who studies the relationship between living things and their environment.

Era: One of the major divisions of geological time.

Erosion: The wearing away of the Earth's surface by wind and water.

Evolution: The changes in plants and animals that over a long time produce new species.

Extinct: Having died out.

Family: A rank of plants or animals that comes between an order and a genus.

Fertilize: To make something become fertile, or able to reproduce.

Fossil: The remains of a plant or animal that has been preserved, usually in rock.

Gene: Part of a cell that determines heredity, what characteristics a plant or animal inherits from its parents.

Genetic engineering: The way in which scientists can alter an organism's genes.

Genetics: The study of genes and heredity.

Genus: A rank of plants or animals that comes between family and species.

Geological time: Time as related to Earth's history (see pages 58-59).

Geology: The study of the structure and history of the Earth.

Hominid: Any human-like creature.

Igneous rock: Any rock formed inside the Earth.

Invertebrate: Any animal without a backbone.

Kingdom: One of the three great groups (protists, plants, animals) into which all living things are divided.

Life assemblage: A group of fossils found as they would have been when alive.

Mammal: Any vertebrate animal whose offspring are fed on the mother's milk from her mammary glands (the breasts).

Marsupial mammal: Any mammal that rears its young in a marsupium (pouch).

Mass extinction: The dying out at the same time of a large number of species.

Membrane: A thin layer of tissue in a plant or an animal.

Metamorphic rock: A rock that has been changed by reheating inside the Earth.

Meteorite: A lump of stone or metal that falls to Earth from outer space; a meteor is the lump while it is visible in the sky.

Mollusc: Any member of a phylum of invertebrates that includes clams, octopuses, oysters, slugs and snails.

Molten: Something that has been made liquid or melted due to extreme heat.

Natural selection: The evolutionary theory based on the survival of the fittest.

Order: A rank of plants or animals that comes between class and family.

Ozone: A form of oxygen gas; a layer of ozone in the atmosphere shields the Earth from the Sun's most harmful radiation.

Pangaea: The supercontinent in which all the Earth's continents were once combined.

Period: A major division of geological time (see pages 58-59).

Photosynthesis: The process by which green plants can make substances such as sugars from water and carbon dioxide (a gas in the air) with the aid of light.

Phylum: A rank of plants or animals between kingdom and class.

Placental mammal: Any mammal in which the young are nourished inside the mother's body through an organ called a placenta.

Plankton: The mass of tiny animals and plants that drifts close to the surface of the sea.

Protective coloration: Warning colours, especially black and yellow, which suggest to a predator that an animal is not good to eat.

Radioactivity: The emission of rays of energy from certain substances, such as uranium.

Sedimentary rock: Any rock, such as sandstone or limestone, formed by the deposition of small particles as sediment in water.

Series: A division of geological time (see pages 58-59).

Species: The rank of plants or animals below genus; organisms in the same species are alike and can produce offspring.

Spontaneous generation: An old theory that life can originate from non-living matter.

Strata: (singular stratum) The layers formed by rock in the Earth's crust.

Stromatolites: Fossil rocks formed by layers of bacteria and blue-green algae; such layers are still being laid down.

Tectonic plate: Large areas of the Earth's crust, on which continents and oceans rest.

Temperate: A climate that is neither too hot nor too cold.

Trace fossil: A track, hole or other mark left by an animal or plant.

Tropics: Very hot, damp regions of the Earth near the equator.

Vertebrate: Any animal with a backbone.

Index

A **Bold** number shows the entry is illustrated on that page. The same page often has writing about the entry too.